IRIS
folding
with iris folding paper

**Maruscha Gaasenbeek
and Tine Beauveser**

FORTE PUBLISHERS

Contents

Fifth printing September 2003
ISBN 90 5877 220 9

This is a publication from
Forte Publishers BV
P.O. Box 1394
3500 BJ Utrecht
The Netherlands

For more information about the creative books available from
Forte Uitgevers:
www.hobby-party.com

Publisher: Marianne Perlot
Editor: Hanny Vlaar
Photography and digital image editing: Fotografie Gerhard Witteveen, Apeldoorn, the Netherlands
Cover and inner design:
Studio Herman Bade BV, Baarn, the Netherlands

Preface

IRIS folding has become one of the most popular card making techniques. You select a pattern, take suitably coloured card and allow your fantasy to run wild with the different colours that you use to fill the pattern. The greater the number of different colours, the greater the choice and the prettier the final result.

In the last year, we have often been asked for more attractive paper. We have now found this paper, and this book, **IRIS Folding with IRIS Folding Paper**, shows you what you can do with it using both existing and new patterns. The paper is shiny and colourful, can be used either straight or at an angle and is supple and thin so that it is perfect for folding. We hope that these excellent sheets of paper will inspire you to make cards like small works of art. You can use this IRIS folding paper to make special cards for special occasions.

Maruscha   Tine

Techniques

The starting point for IRIS folding is the pattern. Cut the outer shape of the pattern out of the card and then fill the hole from the outside to the inside with folded strips of IRIS folding paper. You work at the back of the card, so you work, in fact, on a mirror image. And when you have finished, you stick it onto another card. For a triangular pattern, select three different types of IRIS folding paper where the patterns and colours combine and contrast each other nicely. Cut all the IRIS folding paper into strips in the same way, for example, from left to right. The number of strips you will need depends on the pattern; you will need between four and eight strips. The width of the strips also depends on the pattern and is stated for each card. First, you fold one edge of the strips over and then sort them into the different types of paper. Next, you cover each section in turn by following the numbers (1, 2, 3, 4, 5, etc.), so that the pattern rotates. Lay the strips with the fold facing towards the middle of the pattern and then stick them on the left and right-hand sides of the card using adhesive tape. Finally, use an attractive piece of deco tape or holographic paper to cover the hole in the middle.

The exclamation mark
(see card 1 in chapter 1)

The most important thing is to start with this *basic shape*, because from this, you will learn the unique folding and sticking technique needed for all the patterns. You will notice that you quickly get used to the technique of IRIS folding.

Preparation

1. Lay a cerise piece of card (13.8 x 9 cm, cut at an angle to 13 x 7.8 cm) down with the back facing towards you.
2. Copy the triangular shape of the exclamation mark on the card and cut it out.
3. Stick a copy of the exclamation mark pattern given in this book on your cutting mat using adhesive tape.
4. Place the card with the triangle cut out of it on the pattern (you should be looking at the back of the card) and *only* stick the left-hand side of the card to your cutting mat using masking tape.
5. Choose three different sheets of IRIS folding paper with different patterns. Heart, silver and star IRIS folding paper have been used for the card in the top left-hand corner of page 9.
6. Cut *2.5 cm wide* strips from these sheets of IRIS folding paper and make separate piles of colour A, colour B and colour C.

1. The many different shiny and colourful types of new IRIS folding paper.

2. Cut the exclamation mark out of the back of a piece of card. Cut the IRIS folding paper into strips and fold over the edge.

3. Stick the pattern to your cutting mat and place the card on top of it. Place the strips exactly against the line and stick down the left and right-hand sides using adhesive tape.

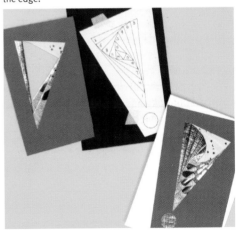

4. Fold the card open from time to time to see whether the patterns continue nicely.

7. For each strip, fold over the edge (0.7 cm or less) with the *nice side facing outwards*.

IRIS folding

8. Take a folded strip of colour A and place this over section 1, exactly against the line of the pattern, with the folded edge *facing towards the middle*. Allow $^1/_2$ cm to stick out on the left and right-hand sides and cut the rest off. By doing so, the strip will also slightly stick out over the edge of the pattern at the bottom, so that section 1 is totally covered.

9. Stick the strip to the card on the left and right-hand sides using a small piece of adhesive tape, but remain $^1/_2$ cm from the edge of the card.

10. Take a strip of colour B and place it on section 2 of the pattern. Also tape this to the left and right-hand sides of the card.

11. Take a strip of colour C. Place this on section 3 and stick it into place.

12. Start again with colour A on section 4, colour B on section 5 and colour C on section 6. The strips on sections 1, 4, 7, 10 and 13 of this pattern are all of colour A. The strips of sections 2, 5, 8, 11 and 14 are all of colour B. The strips of sections 3, 6, 9, 12 and 15 are all of colour C.

Finishing

After section 15, carefully remove the card. Stick a piece of holographic paper in the middle on the back of the card. You can use punches, figure scissors, etc. to add extra finishing touches to the card. Stick small pieces of double-sided adhesive tape along the edges. Remove the protective layer from the tape and fix your design on the double white card. Do not use glue, because all the paper strips place pressure on the card.

Making glitter borders

Fold a narrow border along the length of the strips of holographic paper and add these to the strips of IRIS folding paper. First, stick a strip of IRIS folding paper to the card against the section's *dotted line*. Place a strip of holographic paper on the strip of IRIS folding paper with the fold against the section's solid line and stick it in place. Glitter strips can, therefore, be added to the patterns which have *dotted lines*.

Materials

To make the cards:

- ❏ Card: Canson Mi-Teintes (C), Artoz (A) and Papicolor (P)
- ❏ IRIS folding paper
- ❏ Cutting knife
- ❏ Cutting mat
- ❏ Ruler with a metal cutting edge (Securit)
- ❏ Pencil
- ❏ Fine-liner
- ❏ Adhesive tape
- ❏ Double-sided adhesive tape
- ❏ Masking tape
- ❏ Various punches (TomTas, Make Me!, Media, Carl)
- ❏ Multi-corner punch (Reuser)
- ❏ 3-in-1 corner punch (Fiskars)
- ❏ Punch with exchangeable shapes (TomTas)
- ❏ Scissors and silhouette scissors
- ❏ Corner scissors (Fiskars)

- ❏ Ridge master
- ❏ Photo glue
- ❏ Light box

IRIS folding

- ❏ Strips of IRIS folding paper

The middle of the card

- ❏ Deco tape
- ❏ Holographic paper

The patterns:

Special pre-punched cards are available for all the patterns used in this book (except the basic pattern). Full-size examples of all the patterns are given in this book. You can also easily cut the shapes out of the card yourself. To do so, draw around the circumference using a light box.

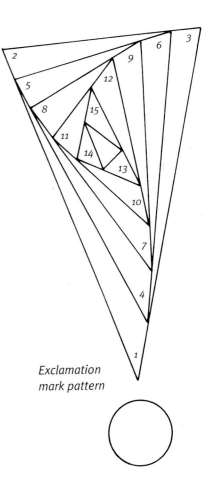

Exclamation mark pattern

Silver

Shiny silver paper combined with mat grey and a touch of pink.

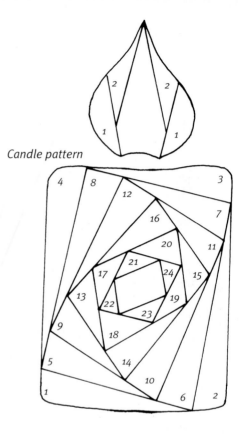

Candle pattern

Strips of brush, roses, bamboo, heart, silver and star IRIS folding paper are used for these cards. All the cards are made according to the instructions given for the basic pattern (see Techniques).

Exclamation mark

rd: white (14.8 x 21 cm) and cerise P33 (13.8 x 9 cm)
Exclamation mark pattern • Three groups of 2.5 cm
de strips of heart, silver and star IRIS folding paper
Silver deco tape

ut the triangle out of the cerise card. Cut the
des at an angle (13 x 7.8 cm) before starting
e IRIS folding. Stick the dot on the card when
u have finished the IRIS folding.

Boat

rd: blue (14.8 x 21 cm) • Boat pre-punched card
3.5 x 9.8 cm) • Boat pattern • Three groups of
cm wide strips of brush, bamboo and silver IRIS
lding paper • Silver deco tape • Celestial corner
issors

ut off the top corners of the pre-punched card

using the corner scissors. Cover the boat and the spinnaker before the mainsail.

3. Teapot

Card: brick red C130 (13 x 26 cm) • Teapot pre-punched card (12 x 12 cm) • Teapot pattern • Five groups of 2 cm wide strips of brush, rose (twice) and heart (twice) IRIS

folding paper • Silver deco tape • Lace corner punch
First, cover the handle, spout and lid with heart
IRIS folding paper. Next, fill the pot with strips.

4. Candle

Card: brick red C130 (14.8 x 21 cm) • Piece of bamboo
IRIS folding paper (13.8 x 8.2 cm) • Candle pre-
punched card (13.4 x 7.7 cm) • Candle pattern • Four
groups of 2 cm wide strips of brush, bamboo (twice)
and silver IRIS folding paper • Silver holographic paper
After completing the IRIS folding, stick it on the
sheet of bamboo IRIS folding paper and then on
the double card.

5. Coffee pot

Card: lavender blue C150 (13 x 26 cm and 11.6 x
11.6 cm) • Piece of rose IRIS folding paper (12.1 x
12.1 cm) • Coffee pot pattern • Four groups of 2 cm
wide strips of rose, bamboo and silver (twice) IRIS
folding paper • Silver deco tape • Multi-corner punch
Punch out two corners of the smallest card and
cut out the pot. Cut the handle, spout and lid out
of silver IRIS folding paper and stick them on the
card.

6. Icicle

Card: white (14.8 x 21 cm), pink C352 (13.2 x 9 cm) and
burgundy (12.5 x 8.3 cm) • Icicle pattern • Four groups

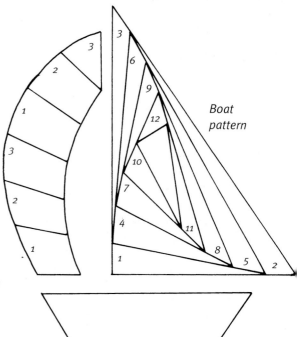

Boat pattern

of 2 cm wide strips of silver (twice) and star (twice) IRIS
folding paper • Silver holographic paper • Star punch
Cut the icicle shape out of the smallest card. Cut
out a suspension eye and stick it on the card.

7. Star

Card: lavender blue C150 (14.8 x 21 cm) • Piece of bamboo IRIS folding paper (14 x 10.2 cm) • Star pre-punched
card (13 x 9.8 cm) • Star pattern • Three groups of 2 cm
wide strips of brush, bamboo and star IRIS folding
paper • Silver holographic paper • Multi-corner punch
Punch out the corners of the pre-punched card.

Red

Different red tints are
combined to make a fiery
card.

Strips of burgundy, little heart, maya, flower,
heart and maze IRIS folding paper
are used for these card.

1. Toadstool

Card: white (13 x 26 cm) • Piece of maze IRIS folding
paper (12.5 x 12.5 cm) • Toadstool pre-punched card
(12 x 12 cm) • Toadstool pattern • Five groups of 2 cm
wide strips of burgundy (twice), maya (twice) and
maze IRIS folding paper • Piece of maze IRIS folding
paper (3 x 4 cm) for the bottom of the stem • Gold
deco tape • Ridge master • Regal corner scissors •
Toadstools from the punch

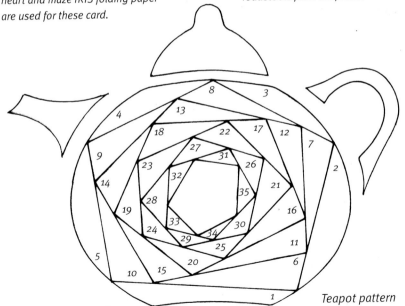

Teapot pattern

Round off the corners of the pre-punched card. Put a strip of maze IRIS folding paper in the ridge master and then stick it at the top of the stem. Cover the rest of the stem and IRIS fold the five groups of strips in turn. Decorate the card with small toadstools.

2. Greek vase

Card: white C335 (14.8 x 21 cm and 13 x 9.4 cm) • Piece of maze IRIS folding paper (14 x 9.8 cm) • Greek vase pattern • Four groups of 2 cm wide strips of burgundy (twice) and maze (twice) IRIS folding paper • Piece of maze IRIS folding paper (3 x 4 cm) for the neck of the vase • Copper deco tape • Carl corner punch

Punch out the corners of the small white card. Cut out the vase shape without the foot. After completing the IRIS folding, cut the handles out of a piece of burgundy IRIS folding paper which has been folded double and stick them on the side of the vase.

3. Tulip

Card: cerise P33 (14.8 x 21 cm) • Piece of flower IRIS folding paper (14.6 x 9.5 cm) • Tulip pre-punched card (14.2 x 9 cm) • Tulip pattern • Five groups of 2 cm wide strips of burgundy (twice), maya (twice) and flower IRIS folding paper • Piece of maya IRIS folding paper (7 x 7 cm) • Silver holographic paper

First, cover the stem and the leaves with the piece of maya IRIS folding paper.

4. Heart

Card: red (14.8 x 21 cm) and gold (13.3 x 10 cm)
• Heart pre-punched card (12.3 x 9.5 cm) • Heart pattern • Three groups of 2 cm wide strips of little heart, heart and maze IRIS folding paper • Gold holographic paper • Multi-corner punch

Punch out the corners of the pre-punched card.

5. Exclamation mark

Card: red (14.8 x 21 cm) and white (13.8 x 8.5 cm)
• Exclamation mark pattern • Three groups of 2.5 cm wide strips of maya (twice) and maze IRIS folding paper • Silver holographic paper

Cut the triangle out of the white card. After completing the IRIS folding, stick a strip of maya IRIS folding paper on the left-hand side of the card. Finally, stick the dot on the card.

6. Coffee pot

Card: burgundy (13 x 26 cm) • Coffee pot pre-punched card (12 x 12 cm) • Coffee pot pattern • Four groups of 2 cm wide strips of burgundy (twice) and maya (twice) IRIS folding paper • Gold deco tape

Cover the handle, spout and lid with burgundy IRIS folding paper.

Bronze

Copper, bronze, brown and shiny gold give the cards a rustic appearance.

Strips of rose, circle, bubble, block, leaf and brown IRIS folding paper are used for these cards.

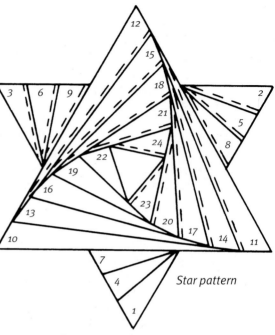

Star pattern

1. Star

Card: white (14.8 x 21 cm) • Piece of circle IRIS folding paper (13.7 x 9.4 cm) • Star pre-punched card (13 x 9.8 cm) • Star pattern • Three groups of 2 cm wide strips of rose, bubble and block IRIS folding paper • Copper deco tape • Star corner punch
Punch out the corners of the pre-punched card.

2. Teapot

Card: salmon beige C384 (13 x 26 cm) • Piece of bubble IRIS folding paper (12.3 x 12.3 cm) • Teapot pre-punched card (11 x 11 cm) • Teapot pattern • Five groups of 2 cm wide strips of bubble, leaf (twice) and brown (twice) IRIS folding paper • Gold holographic paper • Multi-corner punch
Punch out the corners of the pre-punched card. Before starting the IRIS folding, cover the handle, spout and lid with leaf IRIS folding paper.

3. Candle

Card: brown (14.8 x 21 cm) • Candle pre-punched card (14 x 9.5 cm) • Candle pattern • Four groups of 2 cm wide strips of block (twice), leaf and brown IRIS folding paper • Gold holographic paper • Star corner punch
Punch out the top corners of the pre-punched card.

4. Toadstool

Card: wine red C503 (13 x 26 cm) • Toadstool pre-punched card (12.5 x 12.5 cm) • Toadstool pattern • Five groups of 2 cm wide strips of rose, circle, bubble, block and brown IRIS folding paper • Piece of circle IRIS fol-

ding paper (3 x 4 cm) for the bottom of the stem • Gold
holographic paper • Ridge master • Multi-corner punch
Punch out the top corners of the pre-punched
card. Put a strip of circle IRIS folding paper in
the ridge master and stick it on the top and
bottom of the stem.

5. Greek vase

Card: auburn C501 (14.8 x 21 cm) • Greek vase pre-
punched card (13.7 x 9.4 cm) • Greek vase pattern •
Four groups of 2 cm wide strips of circle, bubble, leaf

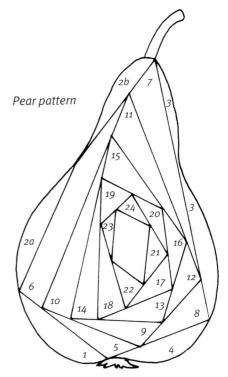

Pear pattern

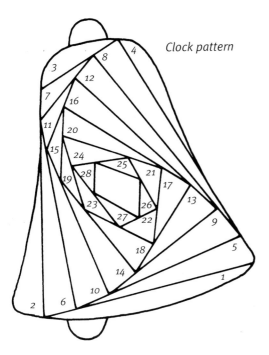

Clock pattern

and brown IRIS folding paper • Piece of leaf IRIS
folding paper (3 x 4 cm) for the neck of the vase •
Gold holographic paper • Carl corner punch
Punch out the corners of the pre-punched card.
Cover the foot and neck of the vase. After
completing the IRIS folding, cut the handles out
of a piece of bubble IRIS folding paper which
has been folded double and stick them on the
side of the vase.

Blue

Blue, either plain or with patterns, combines very well with beige and gold.

Strips of gold, blue, star, leaf, striped and moon IRIS folding paper are used for these cards.

. Spruce

ard: iris blue P31 (13 x 26 cm)
 Piece of gold IRIS folding
aper (11.8 x 11.8 cm) •
pruce pre-punched card
11.5 x 11.5 cm) • Spruce
attern • Three groups of 2 cm
vide strips of blue, star and moon
RIS folding paper • Gold deco tape • Star corner
unch • Stars from a multi-corner punch
Punch out the top corners of the pre-punched
ard.

. Butterflies

ard: white (14.8 x 21 cm) • Piece of striped IRIS
olding paper (13.5 x 10 cm) • Butterflies pre-punched
ard (12.8 x 9.5 cm) • Butterflies pattern • Four

groups of 1.5 cm wide strips of gold, leaf, striped and moon IRIS folding paper • Gold deco tape
Cut two corners of the pre-punched card at an angle. Cover the butterfly bodies. After completing the IRIS folding, cut the antennae

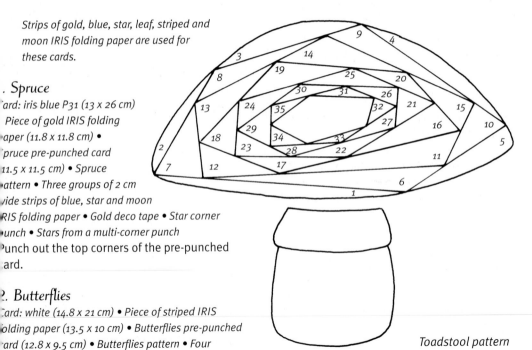

Toadstool pattern

out of paper which has been folded double or draw them on the card.

3. Clock

Card: indigo C140 (14.8 x 21 cm) and azure C590 (13.6 x 9.5 cm) • Clock pre-punched card (11.8 x 9 cm) • Clock pattern • Four groups of 2 cm wide strips of gold, blue, star and striped IRIS folding paper • Gold holographic paper • Multi-corner punch
Punch out the top corners of the pre-punched card.

4. Boat

Card: violet P20 (14.8 x 21 cm) and lavender blue C150 (13.6 x 10.1 cm) • Boat pre-punched card (13.1 x 9.8 cm) • Boat pattern • Three groups of 2 cm wide strips of leaf, striped and moon IRIS folding paper • Silver deco tape • Multi-corner punch
Punch out the top corners of the pre-punched card.

5. Teapot

Card: violet P20 (13 x 26 cm) • Piece of leaf IRIS folding paper (11.9 x 11.9 cm) • Teapot pre-punched card (11.6 x 11.6 cm) • Teapot pattern • Five groups of 2 cm wide blue, leaf (twice) and moon (twice) IRIS folding paper • Silver deco tape • Regal corner scissors

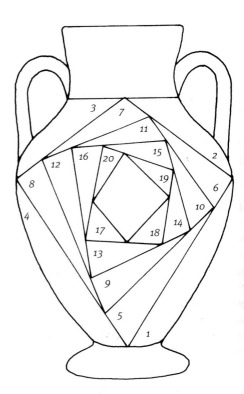

Greek vase pattern

Cut the corners of the pre-punched card using the corner scissors. Cover the handle, spout and lid with leaf IRIS folding paper.

Christmas

Red, green and gold are the most popular colours for home-made Christmas cards.

Strips of green, gold, red, holly, star and striped IRIS folding paper are used for these cards.

1. Clock

Card: white (14.8 x 21 cm) • Piece of red IRIS folding paper (14.4 x 10.2 cm) and a piece of gold IRIS folding paper (14.2 x 10 cm) • Clock pre-punched card (13.9 x 9.5 cm) • Clock pattern • Four groups of 2 cm wide strips of gold, holly, star and striped IRIS folding paper • Gold deco tape • Star corner punch • Stars from a multi-corner punch

Punch out the top corners of the pre-punched card. Cover the bell's clapper and the suspension eye before starting the IRIS folding.

2. Icicle

Card: white (14.8 x 21 cm) • Piece of star IRIS folding paper (14.5 x 9.8 cm) • Icicle pre-punched card (14.2 x 8.8 cm) • Icicle pattern • Four groups of 2 cm wide strips of green (twice), holly and star IRIS folding paper • Gold holographic paper

1.

3.

First, cover the suspension eye with gold holographic paper.

3. Spruce

Card: white (13 x 26 cm) • Piece of star IRIS folding paper (12.6 x 12.6 cm) • Spruce pre-punched card (12 x 12/6.5 cm) • Spruce pattern • Three groups of 2 cm wide strips of green, holly and striped IRIS folding paper • Gold holographic paper

Cut the top right-hand corner of the pre-punched card from the top to the bottom of the card at an angle to the dimensions mentioned above.

4. Star

Card: white (14.8 x 21 cm) • Piece of gold IRIS folding paper (14 x 9.7 cm) • Star pre-punched card (13 x 9.5 cm) • Star pattern • Three groups of 2 cm wide strips of gold, holly and star IRIS folding paper • Gold deco tape • Regal corner scissors • Multi-corner punch

Punch out the corners of the pre-punched card. Round off the corners of the IRIS folding paper.

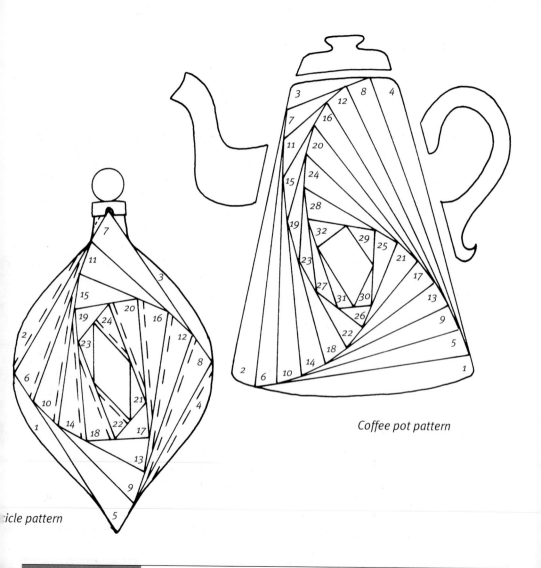

Coffee pot pattern

icle pattern

Yellow

Bright colours form sunny
summer combinations.

Strips of dark yellow/green, pale yellow/red,
flower, maya, black striped and mosaic IRIS
folding paper are used for these cards.

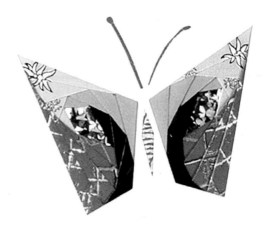

1. Tulip

Card: red C505 (14.8 x 21 cm) and butter yellow C400
(13.7 x 9.5 cm) • Tulip pre-punched card (13.2 x 9 cm)
• Tulip pattern • Five groups of 2 cm wide strips of
dark yellow, pale yellow, red, black striped and
mosaic IRIS folding paper • Piece of black striped
IRIS folding paper for the stem and the leaves
(7 x 7 cm) • Silver deco tape

Cover the stem and the leaves before starting
the IRIS folding.

2. Butterflies

Card: pale orange C553 (13 x 26 cm) • Butterflies
pre-punched card (14.4 x 9.5 cm) • Butterflies pattern
• Four groups of 1.5 cm wide strips of dark yellow,
flower, maya and black striped IRIS folding paper
• Gold holographic paper

Cut the top and bottom edges of the pre-
punched card at an angle. First, cover the
bodies of the butter-
flies. After com-
pleting the IRIS
folding, cut out the
antennae or draw
them on the card.

3. Apple

Card: white (14.8 x
21 cm) • Piece of dark
yellow IRIS folding
paper (13.7 x 9.9 cm)
and a piece of pale
yellow IRIS folding paper (13.2 x 9.9 cm)
• Apple pre-punched card (12.3 x 9.5 cm) • Apple
pattern • Four groups of 2 cm wide strips of dark
yellow, green, pale yellow and red IRIS folding paper
• Piece of green IRIS folding paper (3 x 6 cm) for the

em and the leaves • Silver holographic paper
Multi-corner punch
unch out the corners of the pre-punched
ard. Cover the stem and the leaves before
arting the IRIS folding.

Pear

ard: white (14.8 x 21 cm) • Piece of pale yellow
IS folding paper (13.5 x 9.7 cm) • Pear pre-
unched card (12 x 8.3 cm) • Pear pattern
Four groups of 2 cm wide strips of dark yellow,
ale yellow and maya (twice) IRIS folding paper
Gold deco tape • Regal corner scissors
ut the top corners of the pre-punched card and
ie IRIS folding paper using the corner scissors.
over the stem and the crown of the pear before
arting the IRIS folding.

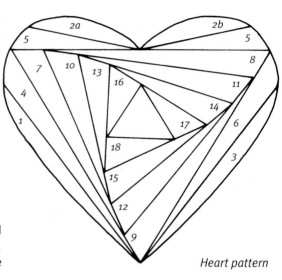

Heart pattern

Toadstool

ard: honey yellow A243 (13 x 26 cm) • Toadstool
e-punched card (12 x 12 cm) • Toadstool pattern
Five groups of 2 cm wide strips of dark yellow
wice), maya, black striped and mosaic IRIS
lding paper • Piece of black striped IRIS folding
aper (3 x 4 cm) for the bottom of the stem
Gold deco tape • Ridge master • Toadstools from
e punch
rst, put the strip of black striped IRIS

folding paper in the ridge master and stick it at
the back of the top of the stem. Next, cover
the rest of the stem before starting the IRIS
folding.

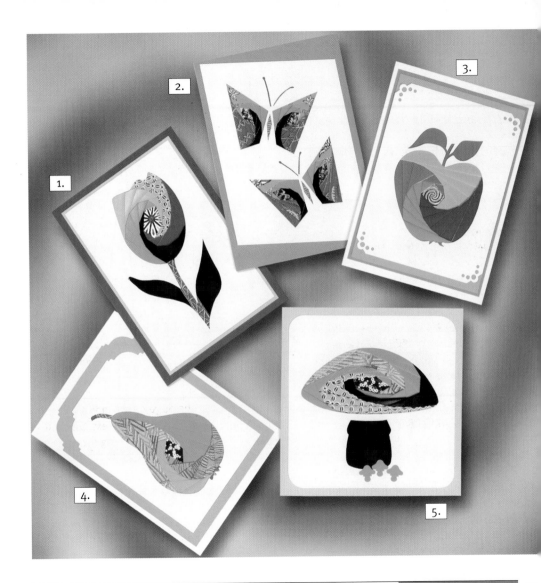

Green

Different green tints, just as in nature, with red as a contrast.

Strips of dark green, light green, diamond, flower, striped and red IRIS folding paper are used for these cards.

Apple

Card: white (14.8 x 21 cm) • Piece of diamond IRIS folding paper (13.5 x 10.1 cm) • Apple pre-punched card (12 x 9.8 cm) • Apple pattern • Four groups of 2 cm wide strips of dark green, diamond, striped and red IRIS folding paper • Piece of dark green IRIS folding paper (3 x 6 cm) for the stem and the leaves • Gold deco tape • Multi-corner punch
Punch out the top corners of the pre-punched card. Cover the stem and the leaves before starting the IRIS folding.

2. Butterflies

Card: green (14.8 x 21 cm) • Piece of red IRIS folding paper (14.7 x 9.7 cm) • Butterflies pre-punched card (14.4 x 9.3 cm) • Butterflies pattern • Four groups of 1.5 cm wide strips of flower (twice) and red (twice) IRIS folding paper • Gold holographic paper • Multi-corner punch • Black fine-liner

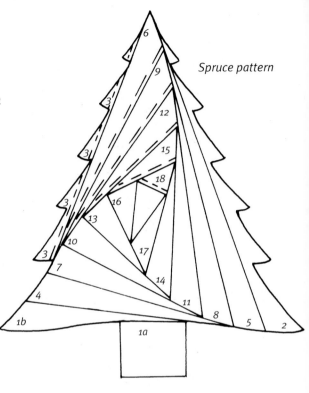

Spruce pattern

Punch out the top corners of the pre-punched card.

3. Pear

Card: white (14.8 x 21 cm) • Piece of light green IRIS folding paper (13.8 x 9.2 cm) • Pear pre-punched card (13 x 8.5 cm) • Pear pattern
• Four groups of 2 cm wide strips of dark green, light green, flower and striped IRIS folding paper

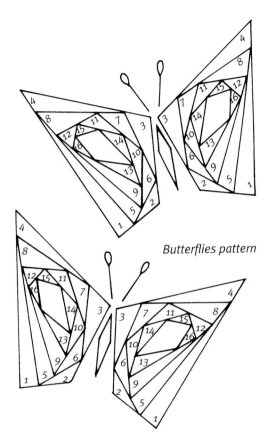

Butterflies pattern

4. Exclamation mark

Card: white C335 (14.8 x 21 cm and 13.4 x 8.5 cm)
• Piece of red IRIS folding paper (14.3 x 9.9 cm)
• Exclamation mark pattern • Three groups of 2.5 cm
wide strips of dark green, flower and red IRIS folding
paper • Silver deco tape • Multi-corner punch
Punch out the corners of the small card.

5. Tulip

Card: white (14.8 x 21 cm) • Piece of flower IRIS
folding paper (14.2 x 9.5 cm) • Tulip pre-punched card
(13.8 x 8.5 cm) • Tulip pattern • Five groups of 2 cm
wide strips of light green, flower (twice) and red
(twice) IRIS folding paper • Piece of dark green IRIS
folding paper for the stem and the leaves • Silver
holographic paper • Regal corner scissors
Round off two corners of the pre-punched card
and the IRIS folding paper using the regal
corner scissors. Cover the stem and the leaves
before starting the IRIS folding.

6. Boat

Card: red (14.8 x 21 cm) • Boat pre-punched card
(13.5 x 9.7 cm) • Boat pattern • Three groups of 2 cm
wide strips of dark green, striped and red IRIS folding
paper • Gold holographic paper.
Cover the boat and the spinnaker before
starting the IRIS folding.

• Gold holographic paper • Celestial figure scissors
Cut off the top corners of the pre-punched card
using the figure scissors. Cover the stem and
the crown of the pear before starting the IRIS
folding.

1.

2.

3.

4.

5.

6.

Burgundy and cream

A classic colour combination which, for the vase, creates an illusion of gold painted pottery.

Strips of cube, wallpaper, streamer, braid, toy and gold IRIS folding paper are used for these cards.

Greek vase (card of the cover)

Card: white (14.8 x 21 cm) • Piece of braid IRIS folding paper (13.5 x 9.8 cm) • Greek vase pre-punched card (11 x 8.8 cm) • Greek vase pattern • Four groups of 2 cm wide strips of streamer, braid, toy and gold IRIS folding paper • Piece of braid IRIS folding paper (3 x 4 cm) for the neck of the vase • Gold holographic paper • Carl corner punch

Punch out the four corners of the pre-punched card. See Bronze, card 5 for further instructions.

Coffee pot (card on the cover)

Card: white (13.3 x 26.6 cm) • Piece of cube IRIS folding paper (12.4 x 12.2 cm) • Coffee pot pre-punched card (12 x 12 cm) • Coffee pot pattern • Four groups of 2 cm wide strips of streamer, braid, toy and gold IRIS folding paper • Gold holographic paper • Lace 3-in-1 corner punch

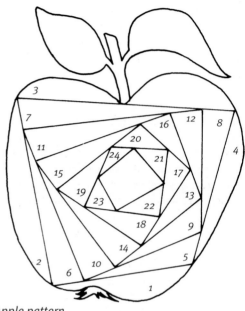

Apple pattern

Punch out the top corners of the pre-punched card. First, cover the handle, spout and lid with braid IRIS folding paper and then fill the pot with the strips of IRIS folding paper.

1. Pear

Card: white (14.8 x 21 cm) • Piece of gold IRIS folding

paper (14 x 10 cm) • Pear pre-punched card (13.7 x
9 cm) • Pear pattern • Four groups of 2 cm wide strips
of wallpaper, braid, toy and gold IRIS folding paper
• Gold deco tape • Bugs 3-in-1 corner punch
Punch out the corners of the pre-punched card.

2. Heart

Card: red C505 (14.8 x 21 cm) • Piece of wallpaper
IRIS folding paper (13.4 x 10 cm) • Heart pre-punched
card (12.8 x 10 cm) • Heart pattern • Three groups of
2 cm wide strips of cube, wallpaper and toy IRIS
folding paper • Gold deco tape • Multi-corner punch
Punch out two corners of the pre-punched card.

3. Apple

Card: cerise P33 (14.8 x 21 cm) • Piece of braid IRIS
folding paper (14.3 x 10 cm) • Apple pre-punched card
(13.8 x 9.5 cm) • Apple pattern • Four groups of 2 cm
wide strips of wallpaper, streamer, braid and toy
IRIS folding paper • Piece of wallpaper IRIS folding
paper (3 x 4 cm) for the stem and the leaves • Gold
holographic paper • Apple corner punch
Punch out the corners of the pre-punched card.
Round off the corners of the IRIS folding paper.

4. Apple

Card: white (14.8 x 21 cm) • Piece of toy IRIS folding
paper (13.3 x 9.8 cm) • Apple pre-punched card

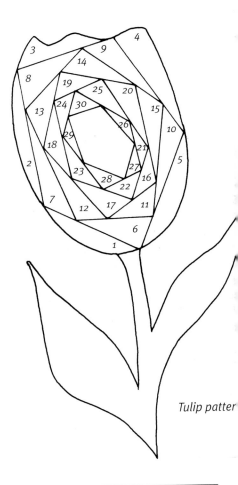

Tulip pattern

3 x 9.5 cm) • Apple pattern • Four groups of 2 cm
ide strips of cube, wallpaper, streamer and toy IRIS
lding paper • Piece of gold IRIS folding paper
x 4 cm) for the stem and the leaves • Gold
olographic paper • Leaves 3-in-1 corner punch
unch out the top corners of the pre-punched
ard.

Icicle

ard: white (14.8 x 21 cm) • Piece of cube IRIS folding
aper (14.4 x 10.3 cm) • Icicle pre-punched card
3.9 x 9.5 cm) • Icicle pattern • Four groups of
cm wide strips of cube (twice) and gold (twice) IRIS
lding paper • Gold holographic paper for the

suspension eye, the middle of the icicle and 1 cm
wide glitter strips • Small star corner punch
Punch out the corners of the white card. See
Techniques for instructions on how to make the
glitter strips.

6. Pear

Card: wine red (14.8 x 21 cm) • Piece of streamer IRIS
folding paper (14.1 x 9.8 cm) • Pear pre-punched
card (13.8 x 9.5 cm) • Pear pattern • Four groups of
2 cm wide strips of wallpaper, streamer (twice) and
braid IRIS folding paper • Gold holographic paper
• Heritage 3-in-1 corner punch
Punch out the corners of the pre-punched card.

Special thanks to:
• Avec B.V. in Waalwijk, the Netherlands, for supplying the IRIS folding paper
• Kars & Co BV in Ochten, the Netherlands
• Royal Talens in Apeldoorn, the Netherlands, for supplying the card

The materials used can be ordered by shopkeepers from:
• Avec B.V. in Waalwijk, the Netherlands
• Kars & Co BV in Ochten, the Netherlands